YOUR KNOWLEDGE HAS VALUE

Mansi Handa

Moral Standing of Animals in Scientific Experiments

GRIN Verlag

Bibliografische Information der Deutschen Nationalbibliothek:

Die Deutsche Bibliothek verzeichnet diese Publikation in der Deutschen National-
bibliografie; detaillierte bibliografische Daten sind im Internet über http://dnb.d-
nb.de/ abrufbar.

Imprint:

Copyright © 2011 GRIN Verlag GmbH
Druck und Bindung: Books on Demand GmbH, Norderstedt Germany
ISBN: 978-3-656-55327-4

This book at GRIN:

http://www.grin.com/en/e-book/265487/moral-standing-of-animals-in-scientific-
experiments

GRIN - Your knowledge has value

Der GRIN Verlag publiziert seit 1998 wissenschaftliche Arbeiten von Studenten, Hochschullehrern und anderen Akademikern als eBook und gedrucktes Buch. Die Verlagswebsite www.grin.com ist die ideale Plattform zur Veröffentlichung von Hausarbeiten, Abschlussarbeiten, wissenschaftlichen Aufsätzen, Dissertationen und Fachbüchern.

Visit us on the internet:

http://www.grin.com/

http://www.facebook.com/grincom

http://www.twitter.com/grin_com

Moral Standing of Animals in Scientific Experiments

Mansi Handa

Abstract

When moral justification of the use of animals in the area of scientific experimentation is well thought-out, we rely on the principles of moral standing suggested by various philosophers. Philosophers try to find out whether animals count or whether animals can be brought under moral consideration. If they cannot be brought under the moral purview, then probably one cannot find any reason that it is morally wrong to use animals for human good, such as using them in painful scientific experiments. This paper brings out some of the principles suggested by philosophers in order for an agent to be considered morally. Further this paper suggests that most of these views do not provide a basis to include animals under the moral purview. Thereby, I put forward a perspective called the 'common sense view' to bring animals under the moral consideration which further implies that the use of animals in the area of scientific experimentation is morally unjustified.

Keywords – Animals, Moral standing, Moral consideration, Scientific experiments, Morally unjustified

Introduction

Animal experiments are used widely to make new medicines and test the safety of certain products to be used by human beings. The use of animals in laboratory experiments typically involves, causing them distress, pain, or mutilation, housing them in cages, and, finally, killing them. Many of these experiments cause serious suffering to the animals involved or reduce their quality of life in many ways.

The chief reason given for using animals in scientific research is to ensure progress in basic and applied biological and medical science. Moreover, it is also argued that if prevention of human suffering is a moral obligation, then the use of animals is unavoidable in scientific experiments. But the pain and suffering given to animals in scientific experiments raises serious moral issues.

The ethical issue that I take up in this paper is – Is it morally justified to perform experiments on animals for human needs? To analyze this, there seems to be a need to turn towards the basis of moral consideration. One of the most fundamental dividing lines in morality is the one that we draw between those who count in our moral considerations and those who do not, or, as ethicists put it, between those who do and those who don't have a moral standing. Therefore, it is required to know whether animals are morally considered? Or in other words, do animals have a moral standing? If they have a moral standing then we can probably conclude that there is something immoral if we use animals in human experimentation.

Philosophers have different standpoints on this issue. Many philosophers argue that humans differ from the rest of the natural world. These philosophers would justify certain human practices towards animals. On the other hand, some philosophers argue for the opposite. These philosophers maintain that although humans are different in a variety of ways from animals, these differences do not grant that animals do not have any moral consideration. I will be engaging myself with the views of different philosophers on the moral standing of animals.

1. Moral standing: General Remarks

An important question to be considered initially is what is moral standing? There is a need to know what we mean by moral standing in order to know the moral standing of animals. Generally speaking, the moral standing of a being determines the extent to which its well-being must be ethically considered for its own sake. In other words, to say that someone has a moral standing is to say that, his or her well-being must be given some consideration.

Claire Andre and Manuel Velasquez (1991) consider that, an individual has moral standing for us if we believe that it makes a difference, morally, how that individual is treated, apart from the effects it has on others. That is, an individual has moral standing for us if, when making moral decisions, we feel we ought to take that individual's welfare into account for the individual's own sake and not merely for our benefit or someone else's benefit.

According to Russ Shafer-Landau (2007) moral standing is its intrinsic moral importance— its ability to impose moral demands on others just by the virtue of its own nature. A person or animal has moral standing provided that we must respect it even when doing so might only thwart our purposes and interest.

Moral standing may or may not entail rights While moral standing is necessary for the possession of rights, it may not be sufficient. So, non-human animals may have moral standing without having any rights (Sytsma and Machery, 2012).

According to some of these above definitions, if entities are said to have moral standing then they deserve moral consideration, or concern, from moral agents. Duties or obligations seems to rests on the moral agents towards entities that have moral standing. Entities that are said to have a moral standing means that those entities morally make a difference. So if animals have moral standing then we mean to say that animals matter to us morally. Duties and obligations seem to rest on other moral agents to protect their well being.

Philosophers have laid down various criteria for moral standing. According to various philosophers there has to been certain essentials that are required in order to claim moral standing. So they offer theories on the basis of which I will try to find whether animals have moral standing.

2. Philosophers on Moral Standing

In this section I consider the ideas of different philosophers on the moral standing to find out whether animals can have moral standing. There are different views maintained by philosophers on this topic. Philosophers have set out some criterion for moral standing. Here I discuss some of them.

2.1. Rationality

Philosophers who rely on rationality as a criteria for moral standing generally hold that only rational agents can be brought under moral purview. Rationality has been one of the most often cited criteria for moral standing This view rests on the assumption of a human characteristic, namely, a characteristic that makes humans different from mere animals and maintains that this is the basis of our moral standing. This can be traced to famous greek philosopher Aristotle's view that rationality is unique to humans. He saw nature as a hierarchy and maintained that less rational creatures like animals are made for the benefit of those that are more rational such as human beings. Aristotle maintains that plants exist for the sake of animals, and brute beasts for the sake of man (Aristotle quoted in Singer, 1990). Thus, according to Aristotle's principle of rationality nonhuman animals are incapable of having moral agency as human beings have. What seems to be drawn out Aristotle's view is that animals cannot have full moral standing, although they might have some sort of lesser moral status.

A similar approach is taken by philosopher Immanuel Kant who suggests that as far as animals are concerned we have no direct moral duties; animals are not self conscious and are there merely as a means to an end. That end is man (Kant in Landau, 2007). It seems that Kant was in agreement with Aristotle as he, too, suggested that reason plays a critical role in morality. In quest to identify the universal principle that determines right and wrong, Kant argued that such a moral principle must be one of pure reason (as opposed to empirical reason) – with moral law being imposed by reason itself rather than by some external enforcer such as God.

Kant had a way of distinguishing between those who do and those who doesn't possess a moral standing. He did this with reference to a being's autonomy and rationality. If someone has both these features then he is a member of the moral community otherwise not. For Kant rationality is a necessary condition for moral agency – "only a rational being has the power to act according to [moral] principles" (Kant, 1785). Only rational agents are capable of performing actions that have any moral worth – that is, only rational agents can be moral agents.

So if we need to look at the moral status of non-human animals in Kant's theory then we observe that animals have no moral standing of their own. According to Kant only human beings have moral standing, and the welfare of other creatures matter only if they are useful to humans.

Kant maintained that animals could not have moral worth as according to him they are not rationally thinking creatures. But then Kant argued that people who cause suffering to animals are likely to use this behaviour on other people also, and bring about a degree of roughness in their behaviour towards other human beings. So according to Kant if a man shoots his dog because the animal is no longer capable of service, he does not fail in his duty to the dog, but his act is inhuman and damages in himself that humanity which it is his duty to show towards mankind. We can judge the heart of a man by his treatment of animals. (Kant in Landau, 2007)

In effect, Kant seems to in favor of a view that animals have some sort of an instrumental value. He says, "... so far as animals are concerned, we have no direct duties. ... Our duties towards animals are merely indirect duties towards mankind." (Kant in Landau, 2007). So, he further argues, "Vivisectionists, who use living animals for their experiments, certainly act cruelly, although their aim is praiseworthy, and they can justify their cruelty, since animals must be regarded as man's instruments." (Kant in Landau, 2007).

But this view that only human beings should be ultimately counted in morality, does not entail that we have no moral obligations whatsoever towards nonhuman animals. Even Kant does not hold that if animals have no moral standing we are permitted to mistreat them in any way. He maintains that we have a duty towards animals as this will help us to develop the duty towards other human beings. He says "we have duties towards the animals because thus we cultivate the corresponding duties towards human beings."(Kant in Landau, 2007)

Thereby according to the philosophers who count upon rationality as a basis for moral standing nonhuman animals morally matter, but only to the extent upto where welfare of human beings is taken into consideration. Well, it cannot be doubted that there is an enormous difference between the life of humans and that of animals. Humans are clearly more significant for the simple reason that they are rational agents capable of thinking morally. Humans have the ability to reason, and this makes much clearer why humans should have more significance in our world. But if rationality is taken as a criteria then aren't we using animals as mere tools for humans. If we use animals for our own benefit then aren't we being selfish?

Moreover, if rationality is accepted as the only basis of moral considerability then the scientists who conduct experiments on animals are morally correct since they are doing it for the benefit of the mankind. Can such a conclusion be accepted? Just because animals are not rationally thinking creatures can we treat them in any way? Kant maintains that animals should not be mistreated but it seems that the reason behind the argument is not so convincing.

However, rationality can be sufficient for moral standing, but it is not necessary. So there are philosophers who argue that it is not rationality, but something more, for instance, sentience is the basis of moral standing.

2.2. Sentience as a Basis of Moral Standing

According to this view, sentient beings, who are capable of feeling pain, have moral standing. Several utilitarian philosophers, Jeremy Bentham and John Stuart Mill, challenged the view that only humans count. These utilitarian philosophers focused on a being's capacity to experience pain and pleasure as a chief concern in question of morality.

According to these philosophers it is our moral duty to maximize pleasure, since every human being by nature seeks to attain pleasure and avoid pain. Therefore, when we make moral decisions, we need to consider all the creatures that have the capacity to experience pleasure or pain and not only those who are rational. In other words sentience is what gives moral standing to agents.

According to Peter Singer a being has moral importance in its own right if, and only if, it is sentient. Rationality and autonomy do not determine the scope of the moral community (Landau, 2007). Those who think of criteria other than sentience fall into the trap of speciesism. Singer claims that both animals and brain damaged human infants are equally sentient, and possessed of identical interests. In that case, there is no credible basis for assigning greater moral importance to one over the other. If one denies this, and accepts that a human is morally more important than non-humans or animals then one is giving priority to one over the other, which is unjustified as both of them are sentient.

This prominent position articulated by Peter Singer, shows no convincing reason to exclude a being who has the capacity to suffer out of the moral considerations. According to Singer then, animal experimentation or consumption is wrong except in a case in which we would be willing to experiment or consume a human with similar capabilities to the animal. "I am urging that we extend to other species the basic principle of equality that most of us recognise should extend to all members of our species. (Singer in Hugh LaFollette, 2002)

Singer wrote a paper titled, "All Animals are Equal", does he mean that humans and animals are equal? He writes, "The basic principle of equality does not require equal or identical treatment; it requires equal consideration." (Singer in Landau, 2007) He further says "There are important differences between humans and other animals, and these differences must give rise to some differences in the rights that each have. Recognizing this obvious fact, however, is no barrier to the case for extending the basic principle of equality to nonhuman animals." (Singer in Landau, 2007) He gives an example that there is no right for men to be pregnant and similarly there are no voting rights for pigs.

When questioned on the basic principle of moral equality, Singer brings in Bentham's view. Bentham wrote, "The question is not, Can they reason nor Can they talk, but, Can they suffer?" (Bentham, 1823) Bentham points out the capacity to suffer as the vital characteristic that gives a being the right to have equal consideration.

So if we consider the sentience view then animals would have moral standing only if they are capable of suffering or have the capacity to feel pleasure and pain. Now this seems to be quite controversial. Are animals capable of suffering in the way in which human beings suffer? If not then probabaly animals have no moral interests and can be treated in any way.

In case of human beings how do we know that anyone feels pain? Pain is a direct experience; only the person who feels it can know this experience. I would say that pain is a subjective state of a person and as such it can never be observed except from some behavior like screaming, shouting or crying. Pain can only be inferred from these external factors. This is how we know the pain of other person. Then can we know that the animals also feel pain in the similar way?

Studies have proved that nearly all the external signs that lead us to infer pain in humans are there in other species too. They also moan and groan in pain. The capacity to feel pain may be different in different species. And even absence of language doesn't cast a doubt on this capacity to feel pain. The state like pain has got nothing to do with language at all. People can even lie by saying that I am in pain, so language can't be the best possible evidence there are other nonlinguistic modes of communication which can work. So in short "Animals can feel pain." (Singer in Landau, 2007)

If animals can feel pain then according to Bentham, Mill and other utilitarians one could possibly defend the view that it is as immoral to inflict pain and suffering on animals as it is on human beings. This idea seems to be convincing to some extent. Animals may not be autonomous, and rational, but they can suffer pain. And that, of course, is what worries us about many uses of animals in experimentation. This brings animals well within the boundaries of the moral community.

But some doubts can be raised on this too. Bentham maintains that there are certain nonlinguistic modes of communication which can help us to know that a person is feeling pain. Language can't be the best possible evidence. If this is so then it can be easily argued that what if I am pretending to feel pain and my moaning and groaning are fake?
Then even non linguistic modes of communication also fail in knowing whether someone is really in pain.

Bentham further maintains that pain is very subjective, if this is so then it is all the more difficult to find out that whether an animal feel more pain than we feel. Lets imagine an experiment being performed on a human and the same being performed on an animal, if pain is subjective then it is quite possible that animals do not feel pain in the same way as a human does. So then it means that we can never be sure whether animals feel pain or not. So may be we need something more than sentience principle to bring animals under the moral purview or to consider animals having moral standing. Thus, I move to the next view.

2.3. Life as a Criteria for Moral Standing

A broader criteria of what has moral standing emerged in philosophical literature which holds that all living things have moral standing. According to this view whether an agent is sentient or nonsentient, it is inherently valuable. This view can be attributed to Albert Schweitzer and Kenneth Goodpaster.

Albert Schweitzer (1929) is well-known for advocating a view called 'reverence for life'. This not only ascribes moral standing to all living things but also accords all living things equal moral consideration. In other words, being a living organism is the one and only valid criterion for moral standing, and there is no hierarchy of status among those things that have moral standing.

Goodpaster also endorses what he calls a life principle, which assigns intrinsic moral importance to all living things. He says "neither rationality nor the capacity to experience pleasure and pain seem to me necessary conditions on moral consiberability." (Goodpaster in Landau, 2007) He further maintains, "nothing more than the condition of being alive seems to me to be a plausible and non- arbitrary criterion." (Goodpaster in Landau, 2007)

The proponents of this view claimed that all life merits reverence. They point out that all living entities, including trees and plants, have interests, exhibiting certain needs and propensities toward growth and self-preservation. All living entities, therefore, have rights to the protection of their interests and we have an obligation to take these interests into account in our moral deliberations.

No doubt, according to this view, animals use in experimentation is unjustified since animals have life. But there is a problem with this view as well. It seems that if all living things have equal moral status, then it is no worse to kill a rat for human experimentation than it is to pull up and eat a carrot. In other words, there is no objective moral distinction between killing an animal, eating a carrot or even killing a human being, since taking of any life is morally wrong.

Now if we try and assess that which view would be better to account for moral responsibility of animals, then it seems that the three principles discussed here seems to be deficient in some or the other way. So does it mean that one cannot account for moral responsibility of animals? May be, we need to pause and think again. What if a new view is derived from the above mentioned views? In the light of failure of the three views mentioned above it seems that we need a new principle on the basis of which animals can be brought under the moral consideration. I call this view as a 'common sense' view of moral standing.

2.4. Common Sense View of Moral Standing

This is a view which I extract from all the above views. Although the above mentioned views have problems to bring animals under the moral purview, but they have some or the other important stance to offer in moral standing.

Let me first put together the three different views discussed above

1. Only rational agents have moral standing.
2. Only sentient beings have moral standing.

3. Only living beings have moral standing.

Out of the three, the third view captures a broader idea of being under the moral purview. But it has a problem as it boils down to a perspective that all living beings are equal. I agree with the third view but I suggest some amendments in this view. Animals and humans, both are living beings, still for some reasons they cannot be kept on the same line. Moreover, none of them can be thrown out of moral purview.

A better reason to bring animals under the moral purview, is to have a kind of hierarchy system for all those who are living. Animals and humans share the property of being living creatures and within this larger property of being living creatures they both differ. Animals and humans differ in their rationality and the capacity of feeling pain and pleasure. Moreover, there are other properties on which they differ like being conscious and aware about themselves. So we cannot say that animals are equal to humans.

But this does not mean that we can treat them in any way. They should be revered as living creatures. At the same time we cannot maintain that animals are equal to humans. It seems that when we are interested in understanding how animals must be treated, there can be no one characteristic, such as rationality or sentience, or anything else, that is relevant to the whole range of ways in which animals may be treated.

It is not that there is no rationality or sentience at all in animals. These properties exist in animals but in varying degrees. The common sense view which I suggest is the view that all living creatures have some properties which they share, probably that is the reason why they are called living creatures. These properties are - being rational, being sentient, being conscious and being aware of themselves and others.

These properties exist in differing degrees in different living creatures. So animals can be brought under the moral purview because of the common sense principle which suggests that animals are living creatures and being living creatures they are to some extent rational, sentient, conscious and aware. Animals should not be treated in any manner such as using them in experiments, since they are living creatures and to a certain level they have rationality and sentience.

I do not maintain that this common sense view is completely free from criticism but at the same time I uphold that this view seems to be the most realistic and common sensical to adopt as compared to the other three views.

Conclusion

This article aimed to find out a moral basis against the use of animals in experiments for human benefits. In this process I discuss the three principles, namely, rationality, sentience and life which are usually used to grant a moral status to an agent. While discussing these, I show some problems with these principles so from the three principles I derive a fourth principle which I call as the common sense principle. The common sense principle suggests that all living creatures vary and to some extent rational and sentient. Thus the thought of vivisection seems wrong to me.

The view that I sketch does not elevate any one human characteristic to a place of supreme importance in determining moral status. Instead in our treatment of animals we should be sensitive to their aspect of being living creatures. But this does not mean that we must treat animals in the same way as we treat humans. They should at least be treated as a life and as a living being should be respected. So animals have a moral standing and this means that it is objectionable to treat them in certain ways, such as using them in experiments for the benefit of human beings.

References

Andre, Claire and Velasquez, Manuel. 1991. "Who Counts?" Markkula Center for Applied Ethics, Santa Clara University, http://www.scu.edu/ethics/ publications/ iie/v4n1/counts.html. Accessed on 5th December, 2012.

Bentham, Jeremy. 1823. *Introduction to the Principles of Morals and Legislation* 2nd edn, chapter 17, http://www.econlib.org/library/Bentham/bnthPML18.html. Accessed on 5th December, 2012.

Kant, Immanuel. 1785. *Grounding for the Metaphysics of Morals* (J. W. Ellington, Trans.). Indianapolis: Hackett Publishing Company.

LaFollette, Hugh. 2002. *Ethics in Practice: an anthology*, Oxford: Blackwell publishing.

Schweitzer, Albert. 1929. *Civilization and Ethics: The Philosophy of Civilization*. London: A. & C. Black.

Shafer-Landau, Russ. (ed.). 2012. *Ethical Theory: An Anthology*, Malden, MA: : Blackwell Publishing ltd.

Singer, Peter. 1990. *Animal Liberation*, New York: Avon.

Sytsma, Justin and Machery, Edouard. 2012. The Two Sources of Moral Standing. *Review of Philosophy and Psychology*, 3(3): 303-324.